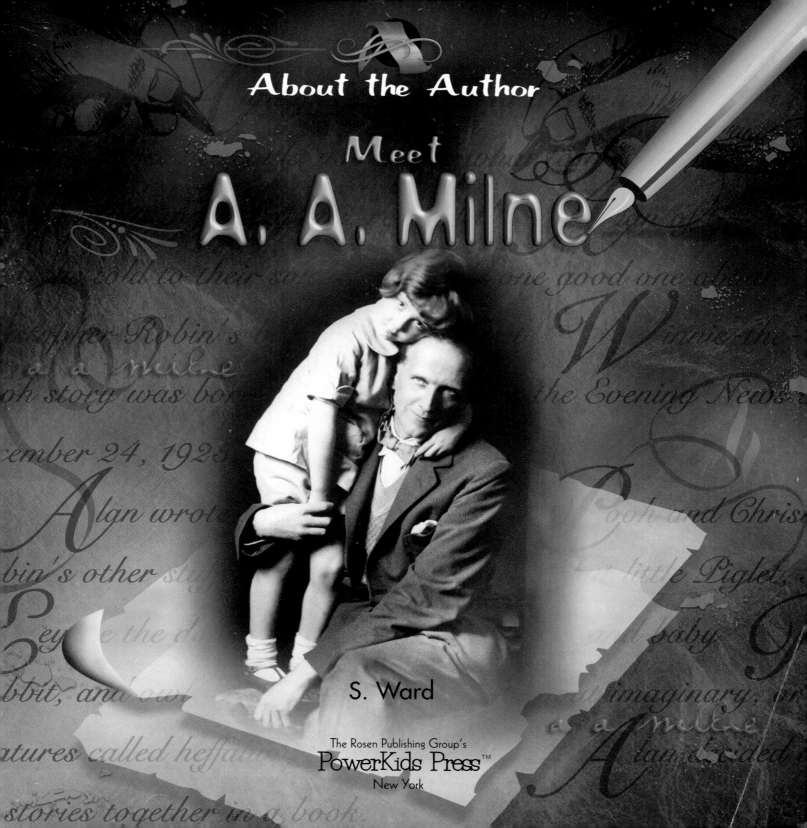

About the Author

Meet A. A. Milne

S. Ward

The Rosen Publishing Group's
PowerKids Press™
New York

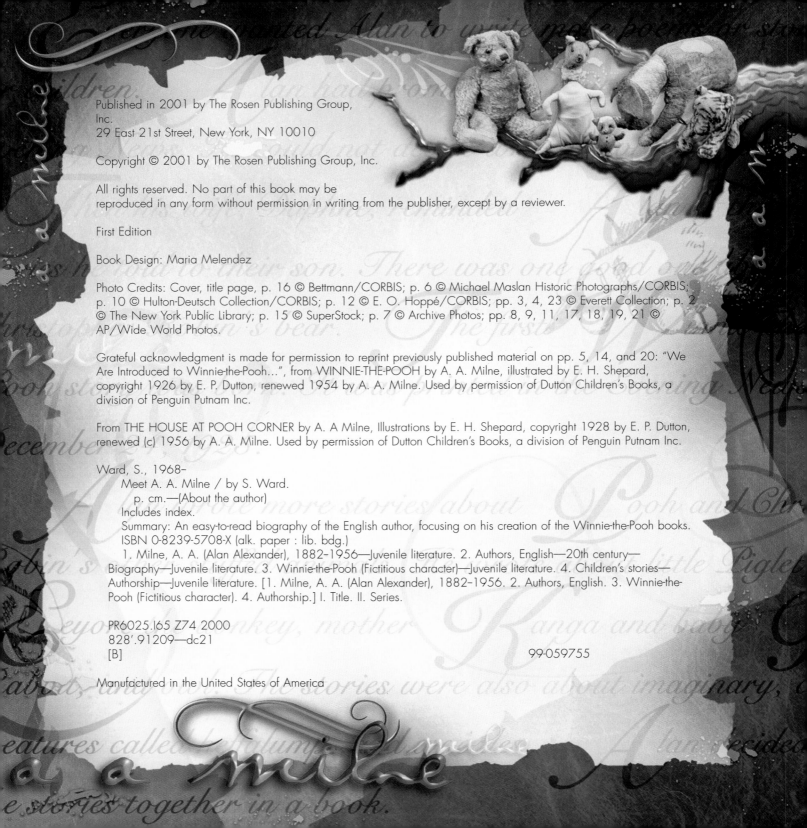

Published in 2001 by The Rosen Publishing Group, Inc.
29 East 21st Street, New York, NY 10010

First Edition

Book Design: Maria Melendez

Photo Credits: Cover, title page, p. 16 © Bettmann/CORBIS; p. 6 © Michael Maslan Historic Photographs/CORBIS; p. 10 © Hulton-Deutsch Collection/CORBIS; p. 12 © E. O. Hoppé/CORBIS; pp. 3, 4, 23 © Everett Collection; p. 2 © The New York Public Library; p. 15 © SuperStock; p. 7 © Archive Photos; pp. 8, 9, 11, 17, 18, 19, 21 © AP/Wide World Photos.

Ward, S., 1968–
    Meet A. A. Milne / by S. Ward.
      p. cm.—(About the author)
    Includes index.
    Summary: An easy-to-read biography of the English author, focusing on his creation of the Winnie-the-Pooh books.
    ISBN 0-8239-5708-X (alk. paper : lib. bdg.)
    1. Milne, A. A. (Alan Alexander), 1882–1956—Juvenile literature. 2. Authors, English—20th century—Biography—Juvenile literature. 3. Winnie-the-Pooh (Fictitious character)—Juvenile literature. 4. Children's stories—Authorship—Juvenile literature. [1. Milne, A. A. (Alan Alexander), 1882–1956. 2. Authors, English. 3. Winnie-the-Pooh (Fictitious character). 4. Authorship.] I. Title. II. Series.

PR6025.I65 Z74 2000
828'.91209—dc21
[B]
                                          99-059755

Contents

Winnie-the-Pooh

It was December 24, 1925. All around London, England, people were reading a newspaper called the *Evening News*. A story for children was making front-page news. The man who had written the story was a **playwright** named Alan Alexander Milne. His story was called "Winnie-the-Pooh." The story was about a little boy named Christopher Robin, a bear called Winnie-the-Pooh, and his other animal friends. The people who read the *Evening News* loved the **characters** and the story. The silly old bear Winnie-the-Pooh would make Alan world famous.

◀ Alan Alexander Milne wrote a story about his son, Christopher Robin, and his son's stuffed animal Winnie-the-Pooh.

"What about a story?" said Christopher Robin.
"*What* about a story?" I said.
"Could you very sweetly tell Winnie-the-Pooh one?"
"I suppose I could," I said. "What sort of stories does he like?"
"About himself. Because he's *that* sort of Bear."
--from p. 4 of *Winnie-the-Pooh* (1926)

First Words

Alan Alexander Milne was born on January 18, 1882, in London, England. His father was **master** of Henley House, a school for boys. His mother had been a teacher, too. Alan had two older brothers. One day his brothers were having a reading lesson. Alan was playing nearby. His father pointed to a word and asked the older boys to read it. They could not read it but three-year-old Alan could. "Cat," he said. His father was amazed. Alan soon learned to read and write well. One of his favorite books was *Alice's Adventures in Wonderland* by Lewis Carroll.

The city of London was a major center for writers and artists.

Alan and his two older brothers, Barry and Kenneth, grew up in central London. ▶

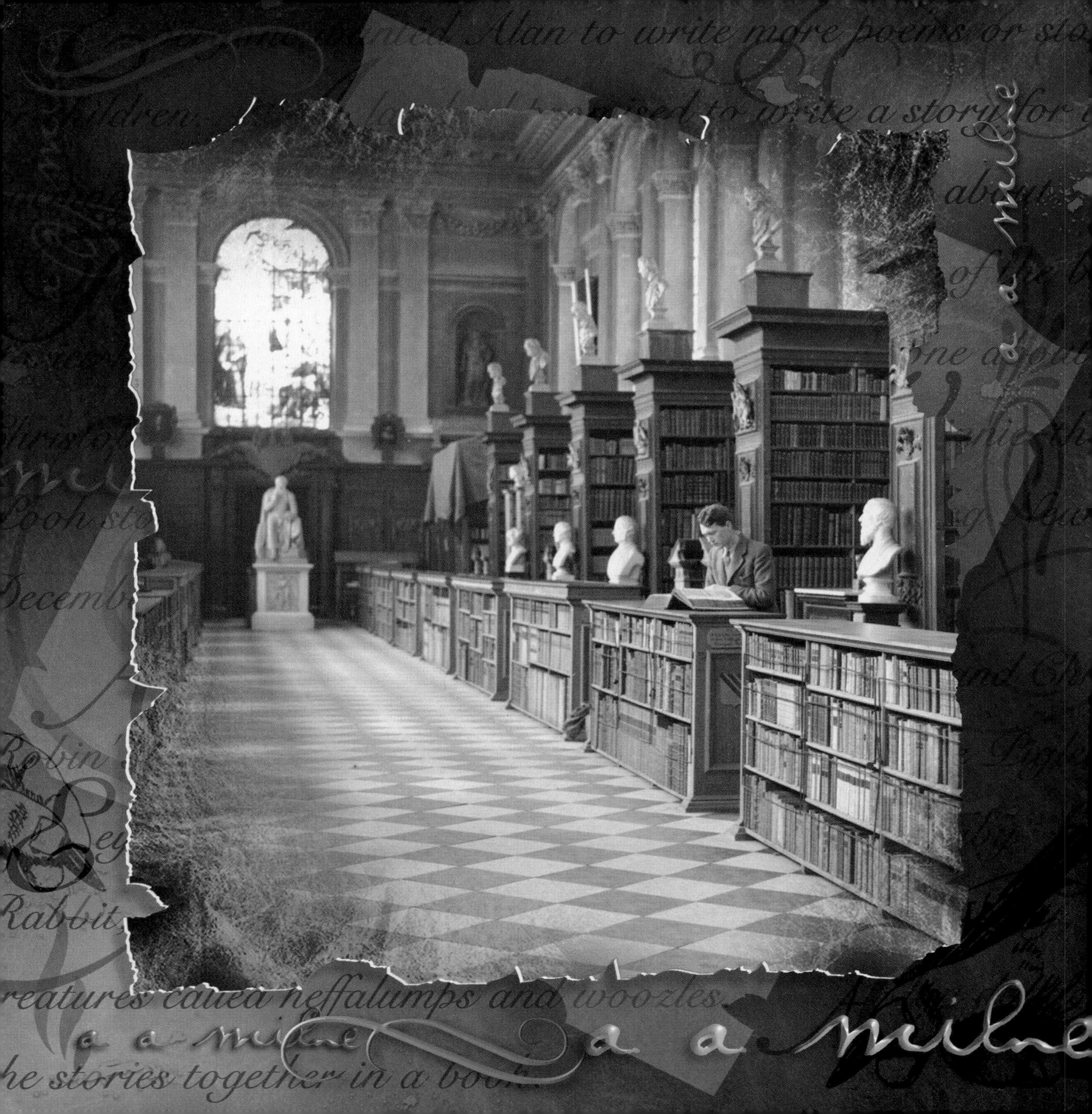

School

Alan was good at mathematics. He also liked to write letters and rhymes, or poems. At the age of 11, Alan won a **scholarship** to Westminster School where one of his brothers was a student. In 1900, Alan began his studies at Cambridge University in England. Alan wrote for a student magazine called *The Granta*. He wrote many funny poems and stories. He decided he liked writing better than mathematics. After he finished all his classes, Alan told his father that he wanted to be a writer. His father gave Alan some money to live on while he looked for work as a writer.

Alan started to study mathematics at Cambridge.

This is the library at Trinity College, Cambridge University. Alan decided that he wanted to become a writer when he was a student at Cambridge.

Writing for a Living

Alan used his initials, A. A., instead of his first name on his work. He wanted his writing to appear in a London magazine called *Punch*. He sent many poems and stories to *Punch*. The magazine printed only two **articles** Alan had sent. By the end of 1904, he had spent all his money and earned little as a writer! Still, Alan did not give up. Slowly, *Punch* printed more of his articles. His hard work had paid off. In 1906, Alan became the assistant **editor** of *Punch*. Each week he wrote something for the magazine.

He also helped choose writings and **illustrations** to print in *Punch*.

This Illustration appeared in Punch *in 1906.*

Alan wrote for the famous Punch magazine.
This cover was printed before he worked as an ▶
assistant editor for the magazine.

FOR THE WEEK ENDING JULY 17, 1841.
PUNCH
OR
THE LONDON
CHARIVARI
LONDON:
PUBLISHED FOR THE PROPRIETORS, BY
AT PUNCH'S OFFICE, WELLINGTON STREET,

Love and War

In 1913, Alan married Dorothy de Sélincourt. Everybody called her Daphne. Soon Alan started to write plays. Then, in 1914, World War I began. Alan joined England's army to help fight in the war. The war ended in 1918. After the war, Alan left his job at *Punch*. He wanted to spend more time writing plays. One of his most well-known plays was *Mr. Pim Passes By*. It was **staged** in London in 1920. Many people went to the theater to see it. Another great event happened for Alan and his wife. On August 21, 1920, they had a son. They named him Christopher Robin Milne.

Alan first met Daphne through his editor at Punch. He fell in love with her, he said, because she always laughed at his jokes and she knew his writings by heart.

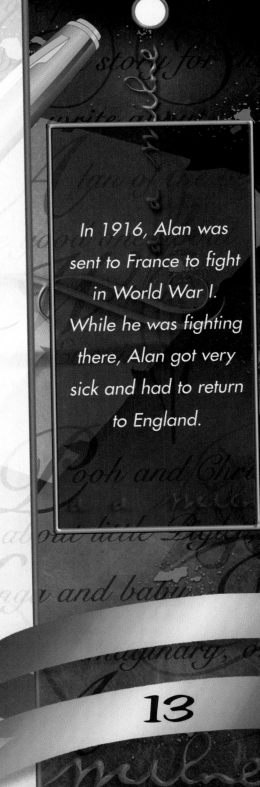

In 1916, Alan was sent to France to fight in World War I. While he was fighting there, Alan got very sick and had to return to England.

13

Playwright and Father

Even though he was busy writing plays, Alan took an interest in his son's life. In 1922, Alan wrote a poem about Christopher Robin saying his prayers. He called the poem "Vespers," which means evening prayers. Sometimes Alan spoke to Christopher Robin's toy animals as if they were real.

One of Christopher Robin's favorite toys was a stuffed bear. He had been given the bear for his first birthday. Christopher Robin called it Teddy or Edward Bear. Readers around the world would soon come to know this bear as Winnie-the-Pooh.

An illustration from Winnie-the-Pooh

Christopher Robin got his stuffed bear as a gift for his first birthday. It came from a London store called Harrods. ▶

Children's Poet

Alan was a busy playwright. He still wrote poems and stories for grown-up magazines. He was not thinking about writing for children. Then a woman named Rose Fyleman asked Alan to write for her children's magazine called *Merry-Go-Round*. Alan gave it a try. He wrote a poem called "The Dormouse and the Doctor."

After this poem, Alan decided to write more poems for children. The poems were put together in a book called *When We Were Very Young*. It was **published** in 1924. Readers in both England and the United States loved it!

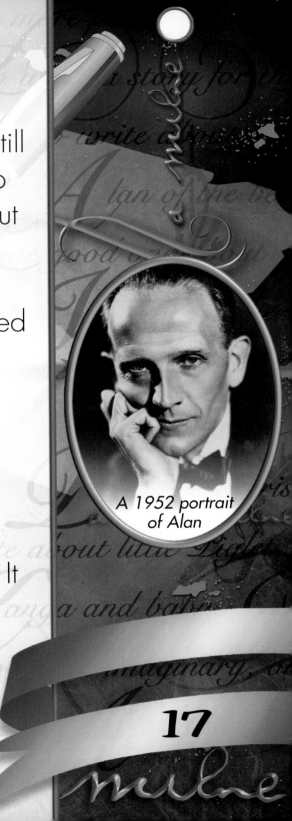

A 1952 portrait of Alan

◄ *Alan first started writing for children after he wrote a poem about his son Christopher Robin.*

A World Famous Bear

Everyone wanted Alan to write more poems or stories for children. Alan had promised to write a story for the *Evening News*. His wife reminded Alan of the bedtime stories he told to their son. There was one good one about Christopher Robin's bear. The first Winnie-the-Pooh story was born. It was printed on December 24, 1925.

Alan wrote more stories about Pooh and Christopher Robin's other stuffed animals, including Owl and Rabbit. The stories were also about imaginary, or unreal, creatures called heffalumps and woozles. Alan decided to put the stories together in a book.

Pooh, Tigger, Kanga, Eeyore, and Piglet were all Christopher Robin's stuffed animals. Today you can visit Pooh and his friends at the New York Public Library. ▶

After Winnie-the-Pooh

The artist Ernest H. Shepard was chosen to draw the illustrations for *Winnie-the-Pooh*. Alan invited Ernest to meet Christopher Robin and his toys. This helped him make the illustrations just right. The book was published in 1926. Alan wrote only two more children's books. The book of poems *Now We Are Six* was published in 1927. In 1928, Tigger appeared in *The House at Pooh Corner*.

Alan kept writing. He wrote an **autobiography**. The Pooh stories were his most famous works. By the time he died in 1956, Alan was one of the world's best-loved authors.

◀ *Pooh meets Tigger for the first time in the middle of the night in* The House at Pooh Corner.

Pooh Comes to America

Winnie-the-Pooh and his stuffed animal friends returned to England in 1969 to celebrate illustrator Ernest H. Shepard's 90th birthday. Today you can visit Winnie-the-Pooh and his friends at the New York Public Library's Donnell Library Center at 20 West 53rd Street in New York City.

Many people wanted to see Christopher Robin's toys. In 1947, Winnie-the-Pooh and his stuffed animal friends visited the United States. They were put on display at Alan's New York publishing company, E. P. Dutton. The animals were given to the New York Public Library in 1987. The library cleaned and mended the stuffed toys. Now anyone can visit them at the Donnell Library Center.

Today, Winnie-the-Pooh is the star of books, movies, and more. Best of all, he lives in the hearts of all who are glad that A. A. Milne decided to write stories for children.

Glossary

articles (AR-tih-kulz) Pieces written for a newspaper, magazine, or book.

autobiography (aw-toh-by-AH-gruh-fee) The story of a person's life written by that person.

characters (KAYR-ik-turz) The people or animals in a poem, story, or book.

editor (EH-dih-ter) The person in charge of correcting errors and checking facts, and deciding what will be printed in a newspaper, book, or magazine.

illustrations (ih-LUH-stray-shunz) Pictures that help explain a story, poem, or book.

master (MAH-stur) A head teacher.

playwright (PLAY-ryt) A person who writes plays, or stories, that are acted out on a stage.

published (PUH-blishd) When something, like a book, story, or poem, has been printed so people can read it.

scholarship (SKAHL-er-ship) Money or help given to a person for his or her education.

staged (STAYJD) Acted out on the stage, as in a play or concert.

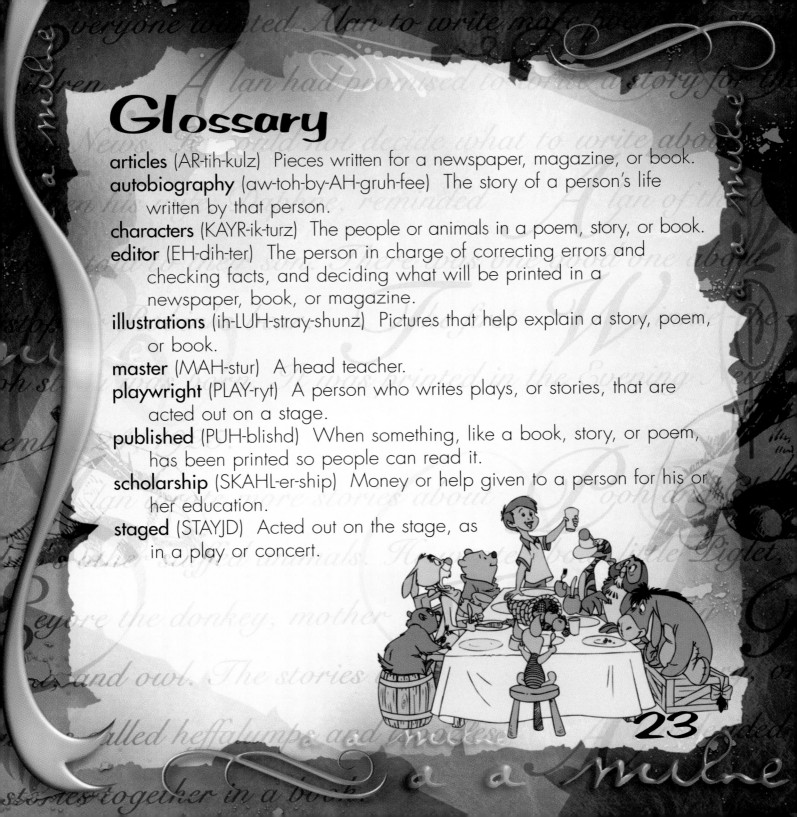

23

Index

Web Sites

To learn more about A. A. Milne and Winnie-the-Pooh, check out these Web sites:

http://www.nypl.org/branch/kids/pooh/
http://chaos.trxinc.com/jmilne/Pooh/